502244 EN
Herons

Grack, Rachel
ATOS BL 2.3   Points: 0.5

LG

ANIMALS OF THE WETLANDS

Herons

by Rachel Grack

BLASTOFF!
2
READERS

BELLWETHER MEDIA • MINNEAPOLIS, MN

Note to Librarians, Teachers, and Parents:

Blastoff! Readers are carefully developed by literacy experts and combine standards-based content with developmentally appropriate text.

Level 1 provides the most support through repetition of high-frequency words, light text, predictable sentence patterns, and strong visual support.

Level 2 offers early readers a bit more challenge through varied simple sentences, increased text load, and less repetition of high-frequency words.

Level 3 advances early-fluent readers toward fluency through increased text and concept load, less reliance on visuals, longer sentences, and more literary language.

Level 4 builds reading stamina by providing more text per page, increased use of punctuation, greater variation in sentence patterns, and increasingly challenging vocabulary.

Level 5 encourages children to move from "learning to read" to "reading to learn" by providing even more text, varied writing styles, and less familiar topics.

Whichever book is right for your reader, Blastoff! Readers are the perfect books to build confidence and encourage a love of reading that will last a lifetime!

This edition first published in 2020 by Bellwether Media, Inc.

No part of this publication may be reproduced in whole or in part without written permission of the publisher. For information regarding permission, write to Bellwether Media, Inc., Attention: Permissions Department, 6012 Blue Circle Drive, Minnetonka, MN 55343.

Library of Congress Cataloging-in-Publication Data

Names: Koestler-Grack, Rachel A., 1973- author.
Title: Herons / by Rachel Grack.
Description: Minneapolis, MN : Bellwether Media, Inc., 2020. | Series: Blastoff! Readers. Animals of the Wetlands | Audience: Age 5-8. | Audience: K to Grade 3. | Includes bibliographical references and index.
Identifiers: LCCN 2018051143 (print) | LCCN 2018051555 (ebook) | ISBN 9781618915283 (ebook) | ISBN 9781626179882 (hardcover : alk. paper)
Subjects: LCSH: Herons--Juvenile literature. | Wetland animals--Juvenile literature.
Classification: LCC QL696.C52 (ebook) | LCC QL696.C52 K66 2020 (print) | DDC 598.3/4--dc23
LC record available at https://lccn.loc.gov/2018051143

Editor: Betsy Rathburn   Designer: Josh Brink

Printed in the United States of America, North Mankato, MN.

Table of **Contents**

Life in the Wetlands

great blue heron

Herons are long-necked water birds. They live around the world. Some herons are called egrets.

Herons make homes near rivers, lakes, and oceans.

Great Blue Heron Range

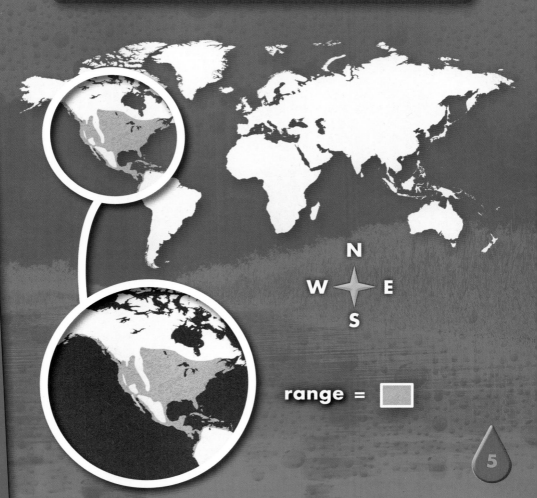

N
W · E
S

range = ☐

little egret
wading

Many **adaptations** help herons live in the wetlands **biome**. Long legs help them **wade** in deep **marshes**.

6

Long, **angled** toes keep herons steady in mud!

grey heron

angled toes

preening

Herons **preen** to stay clean in slimy wetlands. **Powder down** feathers soak up oil and mud.

Some herons use their feet to preen. Their claws are like combs!

Special Adaptations

long neck

sharp beak

long, angled toes

Wetlands often have changing weather. Herons **flutter** their throats to cool down.

10

When it is cold, they spread their wide wings to soak up the sun.

Many **predators** live in the wetlands. Herons often build nests high in the trees to stay safe.

Sometimes herons live in big groups. A **heronry** can include hundreds of birds!

nest

Great Blue Heron Stats

Least Concern	Near Threatened	Vulnerable	Endangered	Critically Endangered	Extinct in the Wild	Extinct

conservation status: least concern

life span: about 15 years

heronry

Herons croak loudly to
warn each other of danger.
They keep each other safe!

Herons like to hunt alone.
Some chase other herons
away when they get too close!

western reef
herons

15

Hungry Herons

Herons hunt fish and frogs in shallow waters.

Their wide feet brush the water to stir **prey**. They watch and wait.

yellow-crowned night heron

16

When fish swim by, herons strike! Special neck **vertebrae** help these birds hunt.

Their long, S-shaped necks stretch far. They easily snatch up fish!

Heron Diet

crayfish

American bullfrogs

black bullhead catfish

Herons **spear** fish with their sharp beaks. Then they swallow food whole.

20

Wetlands give herons big meals. Herons **thrive** in this wet biome!

Glossary

adaptations—changes an animal undergoes over a long period of time to fit where it lives

angled—going in different directions from the same point

biome—a large area with certain plants, animals, and weather

flutter—to move quickly

heronry—a group of herons that nest together

marshes—low, grassy wetlands

powder down—fine feathers that crumble into powder

predators—animals that hunt other animals for food

preen—to use the beak to clean feathers

prey—animals hunted by other animals for food

spear—to catch food by poking a pointed object through it

thrive—to grow well

vertebrae—the bones of the spine

wade—to walk through shallow water

To Learn More

AT THE LIBRARY

Gardeski, Christina Mia. *All About Wetlands*. North Mankato, Minn.: Capstone Press, 2018.

Grack, Rachel. *Wood Ducks*. Minneapolis, Minn.: Bellwether Media, 2020.

Waxman, Laura Hamilton. *Life in a Wetland*. Minneapolis, Minn.: Bellwether Media, 2016.

ON THE WEB

FACTSURFER

Factsurfer.com gives you a safe, fun way to find more information.

1. Go to www.factsurfer.com.

2. Enter "herons" into the search box and click 🔍.

3. Select your book cover to see a list of related web sites.

Index

The images in this book are reproduced through the courtesy of: Pat Stornebrink, front cover (background); cpaulfell, front cover (heron); Joseph Scott Photography, p. 4; StockHouse, p. 6; Agami Photo Agency, p. 7; Malgorzata Litkowska, p. 8; Dennis W Donohue, p. 9; jo Crebbin, p. 9 (bottom); clayton harrison, p. 10; FotoRequest, p. 11; Ondrej Prosicky, p. 12; Chuck Eckert/ Alamy, p. 13; Orna Wachman, p. 14; Dave Montreuil, p. 15; Brian Lasenby, p. 16; Jan Stria, p. 17; scigelova, p. 18; Geza Farkas, p. 19 (top left); Ilias Strachinis, p. 19 (top right); Rostislav Stefanek, p. 19 (bottom); Michael Schober, p. 20; Arto Hakola, p. 21; Collins93, p. 23.